The Christian Foundation

Josh Wilkinson

Scientific and Religious Journal
Vol. 1. No 3.
March, 1880.

Contents

The Influence Of The Bible Upon Moral And Social Institutions.

It is profitable for us to occasionally survey the dark arena where men have played their part, in lonely gloom, without a Savior and without a God. Pagan morality, being without the motives and restraints of revealed religion, and guided wholly by the passions and the lights of reason and nature, is grossly defective. It has no settled standard of right and wrong. It is vain to look, in all heathen philosophy for any settled principles of duty or motives that commend themselves to enlightened minds.

What is the basis and character of virtue? What is the law of moral conduct? What is the object which governs it? In what does human happiness consist? These are questions which have never been satisfactorily answered by the unaided powers of the human mind. The annals of Pagan history show the real results of all their speculations upon these questions. They are comprehensively presented in the following: "They became vain in their imaginations and their foolish hearts were darkened. They were filled with all unrighteousness, fornication, wickedness, covetousness, maliciousness, envy, murder, deceit, malignity. They were backbiters, haters of God, despiteful, proud, inventors of evil things, disobedient to parents, without natural affection, implacable and unmerciful." Their manners and habits were the [082] results of mere whim and caprice when they were not the results of simple love of wickedness. The vice of one community was the virtue of another; and refinement in one was unpardonable rudeness in another. The public festivals celebrated in Egypt are disgraceful upon the pages of history, being accompanied with shameful practices. Egypt was noted for corrupt morals as far back as the times of Abraham. Asia Minor was no better; unrighteousness, sensuality and luxury prevailed. In Greece there was brutal savageness in its most hideous forms; in the age of its greatest refinement sin was dressed up in the finest style. The Olympic, Pythian and Isthmian games, which were kept up to give strength to the body and courage in the battle, were debasing and corrupting to the lowest degree of wretchedness. The ages of ancient heroism were filled up with crime and debauchery. They were fruitful in incest and parricide, and all the dark and gloomy events which were necessary to make up the most fearful picture of immorality. The monarchs of Assyria spent their time mainly in debasing crime and voluptuousness. The brightest and best days of Babylon were notorious for lewdness and accomplishment in crime and iniquity; loaded with riches, they spared no pains and withheld no means in the production of all that gratified their lusts and fed their passions. In Babylon there was a certain well known temple in which adultery was legalized by *compulsory law* for the purpose of increasing the public revenue. The ancient Pagan religions sanctioned and practiced the most detestible licentiousness. Cato commended young men for visiting houses of ill-fame. Such was the very best phase of morals and public manners in the purest state of Roman society. What must have been the worst? The worst! Well, I will give you an idea of it. The Emperor Nero drove through the streets of the capital with his mistress in a state of nudity; and the Emperor Commodus first seduced and then murdered his own sister. Here reason, blinded by lust, was their guide. These people were not troubled with that terrible book called the Bible. Happy (?) state. How would we like to have our homes in the midst of such fellows? Their conscience had no fastenings, how could their doctrines excite to moral virtue?

How much better are the principles of modern infidels? Bolingbroke's morality is all embraced in self-love. Hobbes claims that the only basis of right and wrong is the civil law. Rousseau says all the morality of actions is in the judgement we ourselves form of them. Shaftsbury says, all the obligations to be virtuous arise from the advantages of virtue, and the disadvantages of vice. Have such moral principles ever reformed the world? Do they reform their advocates? Did you ever know a man to reform after he became an advocate of such principles? Did you ever know a man to reform after understanding and abandoning the Christian religion? If any such ever reformed their lives after setting themselves on Pagan ground, by opposing Christianity, I have yet to learn the fact. It is the morality of a wicked world that simply asks for the profitable, and not the right; which inquires not for duty, but for self-interest—for the opinions of men; it is a body without a spirit—a whitewashed sepulchre—splendid only in sepulchral greatness.

Morality rests not upon principles that clothe themselves in various garbs to please the different fancies of the different ages, consulting simply the spirit of the times. Such morality is one thing to-day and quite another to-morrow—it is variable as the seasons. It adapts itself to the occasion—to the hour. It is very pliant—it has no conscience, but is always popularity-seeking. The morality of the Christian religion is very different. In the New Testament we find a morality as pure, lofty and unchanging as its divine author; it purifies and regulates the inner man—"make the tree good and the fruit *will be good.*" The Bible settles the great question of duty. It teaches us that to do right is to do that which is right in itself, from *pure* motives and with a *right spirit.* These two things God hath joined together, viz: the right deed from right motives, and the right spirit. A man's conscience may [084] be satisfied without the right motives and without the right spirit, but that is not enough.

It is not enough for a man to have the right spirit and the right motives, unless he does that which is right in itself. Conscience may be warped by malevolence, selfishness, prejudice, or education, until the man is led to do that which is detestable in the sight of God. The time may come when this man will regret his foolishness, and see that he was wrong, like Saul of old.

Right things may be done from a wrong spirit, and wrong things may be done from a right spirit, but the morality of the Christian religion consists in doing right things from right motives and in a right spirit.

The great motive that governs us as Christian moralists is the fact made known in these words, *God requires it.* You may talk of the dignity of correct morals, of their beauty and virtue, and of the terrible nature of vice, and of the demands of a well-governed selfishness, but all these are weak compared with the authority of the Supreme Being whom Christians love and adore.

If we would reform men successfully we must bring the conscience under the strong bonds of obligation; we must extend the authority of the great Lawgiver over the understanding, over the conscience, over the memory, over the imagination, over the entire inner man. This alone will stop the germinations of sin, and check wickedness in its conception. This is the tap-root of the tree of virtue—the source of virtuous principles, demonstrating the truthfulness of the axiom, "Make the tree good and the fruit will be good." Simple advantage is not the foundation of virtue; it has a nature aside from its tendencies to worldly profit. Otherwise virtue would often cease to be virtue, and vice would often cease to be vice. Anciently there were moral philosophers who plead that utility was the only foundation of virtue. Paul speaks of some who supposed "Godliness was gain." Such a morality would be the most uncertain thing in the world; give it what name you choose, it is mere selfishness.

The Influence Of The Bible Upon Social Life And Social Institutions.

Man's entire nature forces him directly into a social state. He is destitute of the strength possessed by many of the lower animals, and naturally unable for want of speed to escape their attacks, so care for life leads him into the closest alliances with his fellows. Childhood and old age necessitate dependence, and his wants, during those periods, bring him under obligations to others during his strength and manhood. The social state is also necessary to the development of his intellectual nature, and some of his natural affections can be exercised only in such a state. Benevolence, gratitude, complacency and heroism are not exercised in an insolated condition—they are called out only in mutual associations with our fellow-men.

The noblest efforts of intellectual strength and of human ingenuity are made under the most powerful influence of society. Thus encouraged, men have collected armies, founded kingdoms and governed them. In such kingdoms the arts and sciences have flourished in a greater or less degree, and imperfect morals have crowned their labors and lifted their minds as high as their unaided powers have permitted. Such has been the best condition in which the Scriptures ever found the social state. The structure has been incomplete, resting upon no solid basis, and only imperfectly cemented together. Such a state of society has always been a proper object for the modifying and controlling influences of a purer system of morality, founded upon a pure religion.

What has been the state of society in times past without the light of revealed religion? There are evils in the social state where the Christian religion exists, but they were there before the Gospel of Christ visited those places. It is very common for unbelievers to charge the calamities of the social state to the Christian religion, but it is a dishonorable mode of argumentation. The proper question is this: Has humanity ever been well organized in the social state without the presence and influence of the Bible? Has it ever been well governed under such circumstances? Have men respected the social rights and obligations or properly understood them in the absence of revealed religion? Has the religion of Christ been a disturber of the social organization where social rights were properly understood and regarded? or has it set aside the rights and obligations of men in social life where men were enjoying peaceable, happy relations? Does its legitimate influence make men more wicked and miserable? An honest answer to these questions will commend the religion of Jesus Christ, and do honor to him as our Lord and Master. The Scriptures have been the means of establishing institutions which have stood for centuries. Where society has been disjointed and out of order, without bonds or adhesiveness, the Scriptures have been introduced, banishing disorder and bringing peace and good will to man. They have silently operated in the social surroundings and gradually elevated Pagan lands out of Paganism. They refine and cleanse the cruel, giving them habits which make them at once superior to all Pagans.

Look at Rome and Persia in comparison with England and America. The Persian's religion was the best of all the uninspired religions. They worshiped their unknown god in the sun, moon and stars. In two reigning principles they sought for an explanation of the present state of good and evil mixed, which is the perplexing problem that has always confounded unenlightened reason. The Persian's creed only exercised his intellect and gratified his curiosity. It brought no power to bear upon his social relations. Persian history is a mass of crimes, suffering and intolerance. The government was a despotism, and polygamy gave laws to the domestic and private relations of the citizens.

Ancient Rome stands foremost in all that moral culture and philosophy alone can do for social institutions. Its religion was gross in the extreme, exerting an unhappy influence upon the masses, while it was disregarded by the priests who taught it, their sole object being to terrify the multitude and keep them in subjection to the authorities of the state. It was said by a Roman, "Our nation exists more by religion than by the sword." But [087] upon an examination of Roman history you will find servitude, despotism, tumult, revolt, revolution and slaughter, peace and war. The ambitions of rivals to the throne, and new schemes of rulers, often deluged the country with blood and carried the sword to remote and peaceable nations, till the horrors of civil war were realized in almost every part of the world. Every now and then the powers of some great mind, irritated by his calamities, having all the vices and none of the virtues of his species, would rise up and wreak vengeance in deeds which can not be thought of without sadness of heart.

How much better was ancient Greece? How much better are modern Pagan nations? These evils have been extinguished in the ratio of the circulation and influence of the Bible. The relation between the state and its citizens the Bible recognizes as of divine appointment; the foundation of civil government is the will of God. Government is an ordinance of God. "The powers that be are ordained of God." The great author of our rights, life, liberty, peace, order, public morals and religion, has not left these interests to chance, anarchy or the social compact. Rulers were ordained of God, and are rulers, not for their own exaltation, but for the tranquility, virtue and peace of the governed. Where are the Pagan rulers who were taught this great lesson so as to feel its importance? When have they respected the rights of the people? Where have anti-Christian or Pagan nations, in a single instance, been actuated by any motive save the restless, factious determination to sink one tyrant for the sake of elevating another? In Christian lands a free and virtuous people limit the authority of rulers and assert the rights of citizens. In our country a mass of public virtue and a weight of moral influence, that restrains the wrath of man, keeps us from being involved in an ocean of blood at every popular election. We are not repeating the history of Rome in this respect. We have been taught to "Render unto Cæsar the things which belong to Cæsar." The apostles of Christ have enjoined upon us the duty of being subject to the rulers of our land, to submit ourselves to every ordinance of man for the Lord's sake. We have been taught to pray for our rulers. While we do this we can not be rebellious. Who is so blind as to not see that the Scriptures will control our citizens with more benevolence than any other book or any other maxims or set of opinions. When the Christian Scriptures are duly regarded and their divine authenticity respected designing, ambitious, corrupting and aspiring politicians will have but little power to plunge us into crimes and sufferings.

The most important of all our social institutions is the marriage. It is the paternal source of all other relations. There is no exhibition of the divine goodness in conditioning our race that is more significant and lovely. By it our world is a collection of families in which the tenderest affections are cherished and the worst generally subdued. Here there is a community of interests. Here we experience the highest motives to a virtuous influence, especially in forming the character of the youth of our country. The race is continually multiplying and enlarging. What wonderful wisdom was it that consulted its honor, its virtue and eternal destiny by the appointment of the marriage relation? It was the best method upon which human society could be organized. There are narrow-hearted, lustful bigots who would do away the social family compact. They talk about "free thought," "free love," no restraints of law, no protection of the mother save the voluntary. Such has been the custom in a few heathen lands; such is the doctrine of a few modern infidels; such are the habits of a few gregarious communities in Christian countries. In these communities the sexes are taught from the cradle to hate the marriage bond. Such a state of society is poisoned and polluted; is a fearful mass of corruption and rottenness. All moral safeguards are removed. The offspring are thrown out upon the world with no restraints of paternal love and wisdom; no obligations of filial love and reverence; monsters in iniquity, and in a short time equal in crime to those who were swept from the earth by the waters of the deluge or the flames of Sodom. Look then for one moment after the evil of polygamy. It [089] existed for awhile among the ancient Hebrews. Moses suffered it for the hardness of their hearts. From the beginning it was not so. It was a perversion of the ancient institution of matrimony. All the evils of that idolatrous age could not be remedied in a moment; nothing was made perfect until the appearance of that wonderful counselor—*Christ*. He restored the primitive integrity of the marriage institution by revoking polygamy and divorce. Polygamy was never friendly to the physical and mental character of its population. It is demonstrated beyond the possibility of a doubt that it is debasing and brutalizing. The Turks and Asiatics are polygamists, but they are much inferior to the old Greeks and Romans; yet ancient Rome was a long ways from Heaven's will in respect of marriage ties.

The matrimonial institution of Rome was a compromise between the right and the wrong. The institution was considered in the light of a civil contract, entered into for expediency, and protected by the magistrates because it was deemed a blessing to society; by the law of the twelve tables it continued during the pleasure of the husband. The result was that frequent, and often, rapid succession of divorces and marriages took the place of polygamy, and introduced many of its evils.

The private history of Roman ladies of first rank is a succession of marriages and divorces, each new marriage giving way to one more recent. Octavia, the daughter of the Emperor Claudus, married Nero, was repudiated by him for the sake of Poppæa; this woman was first married to Rufus Crispinus; then to Otho; and at length to Nero, by whom she was killed.

Nero murdered Thessalina's husband, and married her for his third wife. Julia, the daughter of Augustus, was first the wife of Marcellus, then the wife of Agrippa, and then the wife of Tiberius. Such examples are found almost without number in the annals of Tacitus. The extent to which this evil was carried may be learned from the poet Martial, who informs us, that, when the Julian law against adultery was revived as a prevention of the corruption of the times, Thessalina married her tenth husband within thirty days, thus evading all the restraints which the law imposed against her licentiousness. What is the marriage bond worth in such a state of society?

Where is the state of society essentially better in the absence of the Christian religion?

The Bible teaches us that the institution is of Divine origin, established by the Lord himself. It inscribes upon every marriage altar, "What God hath joined together let no man put asunder." It definitely defines marriage to be the act of uniting two persons in wedlock, and only two. According to the Scriptures, this union can only be dissolved by crime or death. With great tenderness the Bible prescribes the duties of this relation. "Husbands love your wives as Christ loved the church." This love is not the cold hearted affection that is after the fashion of free-love philosophy, but it is after a model that has touched heavenly hearts, and caused more admiration than all other things combined.

In the ancient dispensation adultery was punished with death. In the Christian dispensation, it is said with *great emphasis*,

"Whoremongers and adulterers God will judge." There is a place of which it is said, "Whoso is simple let him turn in hither, but he knoweth not that the dead are there, and that her guests are in the depths of hell." There is a sin of which the Bible often speaks, pointing the guilty perpetrators to the fact that they have none inheritance in the kingdom of God and of Christ.

The history of Pagan nations is little else than a record of crime. By studying it we may learn something of our obligations to the Christian religion, and our indebtedness to its pure spirit, which has brooded over the darkness of the nations, and brought order out of confusion. It will, also, learn us to value the names father, mother, husband, wife, children and parents; these names were of little value among Romans. In the annals of the Roman empire may be found a record of all that is shocking; a record of [091] all that man can be guilty of; a record of all that an enemy could be guilty of; suspicion, licentiousness, murder, conspiracy of wives against their husbands, and husbands against their wives; children sacrificed by the doings of a mother; families whose peace is ruined by intrigue and violence; men everywhere falling upon their own swords; the wife murdering her own husband for the sake of marrying another; woman practiced, skilled, in the art of poisoning—such is the picture of Pagan life in the most enlightened age of Rome.

Let any man compare society in our country, or in any protestant country, with the state of society under the reign of the Cæsars, and he will see what the Christ has done for our race. The spirit that sustains our social institutions does not grow cold even at the grave, but is felt beyond death. How is it in heathen lands? The sweetest loves of life give way to suspicion and envy; the jealousy of love, the thirst for power and ambition, drives them away, often as soon as the flowers and beauty of youth are gone. Where Christ reigns it is not so. Yet there are those who would have us believe that the religion of Christ is an unsocial, selfish religion. If it is unsocial and selfish to have no sympathy with wickedness, to promote all that is virtuous and kind, pure and true, to take pleasure in all that subdues the malignant and beastly, the ambitious and cruel, then it is an unsocial and selfish affair. If it is unsocial and selfish to take pleasure in that which elevates and moulds character in the image of God, and fits it for angelic society hereafter, then it is truly unsocial and selfish.

Law, Cause, And Agent.

The word law denotes the unceasing, regular order in which an agent or force operates. It should, consequently, be distinguished from cause or efficiency; it being only the manner, or mode, according to which an agent or cause manifests itself. Therefore law is neither cause or agent. Yet it implies an agent, or an energy; for without these law is nothing—does nothing. The laws of nature had no existence until nature existed. That is to say, the laws of water did not exist until water existed, etc. So it is easy to perceive the truth that the laws of nature created nothing. Nature is said to be the aggregate of everything; therefore nature created nothing. The laws of nature, being the rules according to which effects are produced, demonstrate the existence of a cause or agent which operates. As the rules of navigation never steered a ship, so the law of gravity never moved a planet. A bare order or law of nature was not the cause of nature. To confound order or law with cause is to speak unadvisedly—unintelligently; it is perfectly irrational. Would you cut off executive authority in a government and continue its existence without a person or society to exercise, judge and execute according to law?

To say the world is governed by the laws of nature, without rising up in our thoughts to the efficient cause and superior reason, or, that which is always implied in the term law, viz., a legislator and executive putting in force, is to play the Atheist and take things by halves; is to suppose the laws of nature are beings, and imagine fabulous divinities in ignoring or setting aside the Christian's God, who is the source of all the laws of nature, and who governs all things according to them. "The laws of nature are the art of God." Without the presence of such an agent—one who is conscious of all upon which the laws of nature depend—producing all that the laws prescribe—the laws themselves could have no existence. The intelligence, or, if you prefer it, cause, which gives the laws of nature their power, and by which they are kept in action, must be everywhere present and always present; otherwise the whole machinery of nature would be deranged—inertia is a property of matter. The universal presence of God is the one great and overwhelming condition of the existence of life and motion throughout the vast universe of nature. The laws of matter are the laws which he has prescribed for his own action. His presence is the essential condition of any natural course of events in the history of matter. [093] His universal agency is the only organ of power adequate to the accomplishment of the wonders of nature—the only solution of its great problems which lies within the reach of human reason. Some fools still say in their hearts there is no God.

One of Newton's great laws of motion is, that a body must continue forever in a state of rest, inertia being a property of matter, or being put in motion continues forever in a straight line, if it be not disturbed by the action of an *external* cause.

Now let us apply this law to our planet, as a body, and see the result. What is the first necessary conclusion to which we are driven? Ans. Some external agency or cause put our planet in motion. What is the second conclusion? Ans. Some agent or cause controls its motion causing it to depart from a straight line. Do you say the cause is in the influence of other planets? Well, suppose, for the sake of the argument, we admit it, are we then through with the problem? No. We have only moved the difficulty one step backward. We can see how one billiard ball may set another in motion, but it is only thinkable upon the supposition that there was an agent behind the ball which put the second ball in motion. What put the first ball in motion? Did it put itself in motion? No. The law is this: A body must remain forever at rest without some external agency to put it in motion. Now, you step out from our planet to its nearest neighbor, and from thence to the next, and so on till you get to the furthest limits of matter—carry along with you the idea that one planet has put another in motion until you arrive at the last one thinkable, and then ask yourself this question: Is inertia a property of matter here? Is the law of motion, already quoted, a law of motion here? If it is, then, of necessity, science demands an agent outside of planets, or behind the whole of them, to put them in motion, and to control them while in motion in order to carry them forward in *circles*—do you see? "But the fool says in his heart there is no God."

[094]

The Inconsistency Of Modern Unbelievers Or Materialists.

The materialistic unbeliever is necessarily bound up in a contradiction from which there is no escape short of a denial of the eternity of matter, space and duration, on the one hand, or a denial of the materialistic philosophy, upon the other.

His reasoning is this: Space exists. I know it exists. I can't set bounds to space, therefore it is infinite.

Matter exists. I know it exists. I can't annihilate matter, therefore matter is eternal.

Duration is. I know it is. I can't set limits to it; therefore duration is infinite.

Now, it is easy to discover that the conclusion in each case rests upon two thoughts. First, Conscious knowledge expressed in the phrase "I know." Secondly, Want of power to set bounds to space, to limit duration and annihilate matter.

The other and contrary side is brought up in the following arrangement: Mind exists. I know it exists. I can't set limits to mind; therefore mind is infinite, mind is eternal.

Life exists. I can't comprehend or set limits to life; therefore life is infinite, life is eternal.

The time was when there was no life or mind associated with or in matter, the matter belonging to our planet. From whence came life? From whence came mind? Do you say from the laws of nature? Well, laws are rules by which agents act. Laws are nothing unless there is an agent to act in harmony with them or by them. There is consequently something lying behind the laws of nature, acting by them. What is that something? Do you say it is force? Force is the manifestation of energy—a mere attribute. There is something behind energy, to which it belongs. Do you say it is matter? Inertia is a property of matter? From whence came life and mind? The time was when they were not here.

You unbelievers say it is scientific to reason from your own conscious knowledge upon the line of physical elements, as well [095] as space and duration, to the ideas of infinite matter, space, and duration. Do you not know that there is also a line of vital and mental forces? Why is it that you do not consider men equally scientific who reason upon that line from conscious knowledge to the idea of an ever-living, all-powerful intelligence? Power is a matter of conscious knowledge. Can you set limits to it? No, never! Then power is infinite. Let us ever remember there is no life without antecedent life; no mind without antecedent mind; and no matter without antecedent substance. Where does power come from? Can you tell? If you are a Theist you can. If you are an Atheist you can't. Unbelievers say the Infinite One, if there be such, can not be revealed to man. This conclusion is rested upon the assumption that the finite can not comprehend the infinite. This is regarded as a complete overthrow of revealed religion. Can nothing be revealed to me unless I can comprehend it? Can I know nothing without comprehending it? I know load-stone, but do I comprehend it? I know electricity, but do I comprehend it? I am conscious of life and mind, but do I comprehend either? We know that matter, of itself, is inert, dead, and yet it lives. But this is our difficulty: How does it come to live? We know it lives, but do we comprehend the fact? We know enough about a great many incomprehensible things for all practical purposes. Do you unbelievers know the *unknown*? If you don't, might it not be well to quit talking about it? Your language is at fault. You are no more competent to talk about the *unknown* than we Christians. Turn that word *unknown* out of doors and adopt the word *incomprehensible*, and then talk about it, for it is revealed to all who talk about it. You and I apprehend the INFINITE ONE. You talk about infinite space, infinite duration, infinite substance. Yes, and I talk about infinite life, infinite power and infinite mind. We all know there are infinities in existence. We apprehend them, knowing enough about them for all practical life purposes. You talk about the infinities known in science, and I talk about the infinities known in religion. After all our reasoning may it not be true that mind is infinite in its capacities? May it not, in the future, comprehend many things which are now incomprehensible? My increase of knowledge, consequent upon the capacities of my mind, enables me to comprehend a great deal that I could not comprehend a few years ago. If I could not have apprehended those things prior to comprehending them, I never would have learned enough about them to comprehend them. I always apprehend a thing, know it is, before I begin to investigate it. Now, I know God, but I do not comprehend him. He is too great in his majesty for my present knowledge. I may never comprehend him, still I apprehend him and know enough for all practical life purposes. I believe that I shall know a great deal more about him in the future; yes, more even in this life, if I am only faithful in "going on to know the Lord."

Materialism In Its Bearings Upon Person And Personality.

Personality is individuality, existing in itself, but with a nature as its ground.—*Coleridge.*

Paley says: The seat of intellect is a person.

Lock says: Person stands for a thinking, intelligent being, that has reason and reflection, and can consider itself as itself, ... which it does only by that consciousness which is inseparable from thinking, and as it seems to me essential to it, it being impossible for any one to perceive without perceiving that he does perceive.

Henry Taylor says: The quality of intelligence is essential in order to person. That which is not intelligent we call a thing, and that which is intelligent we call a person. By the word person we therefore mean a thing or substance that is intelligent, or a conscious being; including in the word the idea both of the substance and its properties together.

Oldfield says: Person is a subsisting substance or "*suppositum*," endued with reason as a man is, that is capable of religion.

Thompson says: Person as, applied to Deity, expresses the definite and certain truth that God is a living being and not a dead material energy.

Jouffroy says: Personality, in jurisprudence, denotes the capacity of rights and obligations which belong to an intelligent will.

A person is a being who is intelligent and free. Every spiritual and moral agent, every cause which is in possession of responsibility and consciousness, is a person.

Webster says: Person is an individual human being consisting of body and soul. We apply the word to living beings possessed of a rational nature; the body when dead is not called a person.

The Biblical ground nature of the word person is in these words: "What man knoweth the things of a man but the spirit of man which is in him."

Intelligence is an essential attribute of person, but it is not a property of matter. If intelligence is a property of matter, then the distinction between person and thing is of a necessity a distinction without a difference. But no greater absurdity could possess the human mind for one moment than the thought that intelligence is a property or quality of matter. Nothing short of the fact expressed in Bible language that the spirit of man is a gift from God, will account for the distinction between person and thing. Man in his physical nature is enslaved to the laws of physical nature in common with all organized things; is subject to the laws that control matter. The law of organic existence is such that he can not live without a continual supply of food, which the nutritive process continually provides in order to make up for the wastage consequent upon disintegration of parts. But there are impassible limits fixed to the nutritive process by the most certain of all laws, viz: those of gravity and chemical action. To abolish these laws would insure the destruction of all organic existence, because it would be the abrogation of the essential conditions of organized being. Yet it is true that when a certain point is reached a change and dissolution of the molecules always takes place, and this change is the sure introduction of death. Hence, nothing short of union with God, through his own appointed means, by which he brings his own omnipotence to bear for the purpose of controlling the essential condition of organic existence, could ever be an antidote of death. Man in his original innocence enjoyed such means in the fruit of the tree of life. Being removed from this he dies by the essential laws of his existence. So man in his physical nature is enslaved in common with all things that are under the reign of physical laws. Yet he is a free intelligence. He is conscious of his freedom. There is in his history an abundance of evidence to demonstrate his freedom. There is also a sufficient amount of evidence to demonstrate the slavery of his physical nature. But why refer to evidence here? These are facts of consciousness. Man's personality is, in view of all that has been said, grounded upon his mental or spiritual nature, which was always free, otherwise his identity is lost forever in the grave. I have said, if the attributes of person are properties of matter, there is no distinction between persons and things; in such a case persons would be things and things would be persons. Here it is easy to see that the materialistic philosophy upon the subject of man's identity changes the ground nature of personality, and destroys all distinction between persons and things.

Was It Right?

Scientists are the last men upon the earth that should deal unfairly with the Bible. They profess to investigate, to analyze, to demonstrate. In one word, they profess to be in the lead of thought in a very progressive age; therefore we expect just a little more from them than from the unscientific. But, alas! many of them are mere socialists, and many who are scientists have never investigated the Bible, do not understand its facts, and are also averse to its claims.

[099]

"Science takes account of phenomenon, and seeks to understand its law." Now let us apply the test to some of the objectionable facts of the Bible, and note the result.

Moses said to the children of Israel, Understand, therefore, this day, that the Lord thy God is he who goeth over before thee. As a consuming fire he shall destroy them, and he shall bring them down before thy face; so shalt thou drive them out and destroy them quickly, as the Lord hath said unto thee. Deut. 9: 3. This language has reference to the inhabitants of the land of Canaan. Their wickedness appears in the following quotations. Deut. 12: 29, 31. When the Lord thy God shall cut off the nations from before thee, take heed to thyself that thou be not snared by following them, and that thou inquire not after their gods, saying, How did these nations serve their gods? even so will I do likewise. Thou shalt not do so unto the Lord thy God: for *every abomination* to the Lord, which he hateth, have they done unto their gods; for even their sons and their daughters they have burnt in the fire to their gods. The destruction of these idolators, who were burning their own sons and daughters in the fire, furnishes unbelievers and skeptics with a great deal of capital, which can be used with ignorance, but not with intelligence.

What was the law governing in the case? The answer is in these words: The course of conduct which is for the greatest good of the greatest number is right. This law is known in the science of civil government. It has its place in the history of all civil governments. Without it we are unable to account for the facts known in the history of our own government. It is a law that lies at the foundation of all moral and social institutions. Those wicked tribes in the land of Canaan, and upon its borders, were in the way of the establishment of any civil institution. It is to be remembered, also, that the children of Israel did not forfeit their rights in the land by going down into Egypt in the time of a famine.   [100]

The land was theirs by right of preoccupancy and by gift. Upon their return from Egypt they found no civil institutions in the land, but, on the contrary, the people were burning their own children in the fire. They were also guilty of every abominable thing that was hateful in the sight of God. They were utterly unqualified for citizenship in any civil state, so they were cut off as cankers upon the body.

To the same end, the greatest good to the greatest number, our government has cut off thousands of better men. When the children of Israel went into the idolatrous worship of those wicked heathen and burned their sons and daughters in the fire to Molech, the Lord gave them statutes and laws which were not good, and whereby they might not live. He served them right. How can civil government be perpetuated, or even exist, in the midst of such heathenish idolatry? If infidel objections, based upon the destruction of such wicked hordes as were put to death in Canaan, are worth anything they are worth enough to sanction, by the protection of civil government, all manner of abominations that are known among barbarous heathen.

These enemies of God and the Bible talk as though such an outrage as burning sons and daughters in the fire to idol gods should not be visited with such punishment. Would they do any better? Could they manage such barbarous murderers better for the general good? If it was possible for a civil government to allow such characters the rights of citizenship it would be at the expense of giving license to all other crimes, for there are no crimes greater in their heinousness than *murderous idolatry*. If infidels ever get the power in this or any other civil government, and carry out the spirit of their lectures against the God of the Bible, the government will soon come to an end, and crime of every grade and character will prevail. American citizens have seen many better men than old Amalek die. It is possible that a few unbelievers who were out in the late civil war have seen better men die. It is possible that a few unbelieving colonels have killed better men upon Southern battle-fields, and it is possible that a few of them are traveling over the country abusing Moses and the God of the Bible for putting worse men to death.

[101]

Let us ever remember that the eternal laws of right, sometimes, necessitate the destruction of human life. The greatest good of the greatest number is an object that should always govern the action of a nation. This law should never be disregarded. Murder, having no connection with the general good, is a very different thing. When an individual is put to death by an individual to gratify malice its relations are not with the general good.

All sensible men, who are acquainted with the Bible, know that the facts of the Bible, known in the ancient wars of the nation of Israel, like the facts known in the wars of our own nation, would look terrible in the relations of murder. Things out of their relations are always ugly. A man and a woman living together as husband and wife outside of the marriage relation, would be in adultery, while others living in the same manner, but inside of the matrimonial relation, would be in a grand and praiseworthy union. Why is it that sensible men will wrest the Scriptures, taking things out of their proper relations, and do it to their own condemnation? "Happy is the man who condemneth not himself in that thing which he alloweth."

It Only Needs To Be Seen, And Its Ugliness At Once Appears.

"Are such shams of rights, as caucus-and-ballot-boxism can give us, worth spending any more time and money and agitation upon? I ask, and I appeal to what has been most lyingly named free government in Greece, Rome, England, Venice, France, the United States, and wherever else it has been attempted to *make permanent the crisis stage* of progress which marks the departure from monarchy. No, my friends, art-liberty *alone* can be of any avail.... By art-liberty, my friends, I mean the *practical application* of *all* science and art *systemized* as fast as unfolded. The only law which can govern a free state must [102] be *discovered*; it must be drawn from the *whole of science and art*—not 'enacted.' Human law can no more be 'enacted' than can physical law." ... "Man's leaders must find out how to satisfy man's highest aspirations, instead of catering for his prejudices; instead of confirming him, by flattery and cajolery, in his false, supernaturalistic notions; instead of studying the trickery of representing and plundering him. And they will rapidly find this out, as soon as a knowledge (already attained) of the *unity of science* spreads among them, and along with it its correllate, that all mankind are one organism, no individual of which can be indifferent to *each* and *all* of the others. Enlightened, far-seeing, *all-benefiting selfishness* will then take the place of short-sighted, suicidal, penny-wise pound-foolish cunning; and that barricade of hypocrisy, duty, that most fallible of all guides, conscience, and 'virtue' and 'vice,' those most unscientific and mischievous expressions that have ever crept into the vocabulary of human folly, will be obsolete."

Here is the outcome of the liberty that infidels talk so much about. "Art-liberty" is to ANNIHILATE CONSCIENCE and the distinction between virtue and vice so completely that there will be no more use for the words, "they will be obsolete." "All benefiting selfishness will then govern humanity." Reader, are you prepared for such a state of society? "If all *contracts* in accordance with present 'law' were fulfilled to the letter, and if all the '*duties*' enjoined by present moralism were unflinchingly performed, and if all which 'virtue' styles 'vice' was entirely abstained from, and if what is now 'free trade' according to 'law,' had a 'fair field,' how long would it take a millionth of the earth's inhabitants to accumulate *all* its wealth? In my opinion, it would not take ten generations to produce that reign of 'law,' 'principle,' 'morality,' 'virtue' and 'free trade,' or mind-your-own-business, and every-one-for-himself-ism, on the earth." Are infidels down on law, down on virtue, down on principle, down on morality, etc.? *It seems so.* "But there must be no stealing, swindling or robbery, as *legally defined, on any* account; and there must be no sexual intercourse out of the bonds of monogamy, *even for bread*, and, above all, there must be no acts, or even words of *treason*. The laboring man and the laboring woman must patiently and slowly (nay, not very slowly, I'm thinking,) die on such wages as they who, *in perfect security*, hold all the wealth, choose to give; and those out of work must brave martyrdom to 'principle,' by starving straightway, unless they can obtain a 'permit' to drag out a few months, possibly years, in sack-cloth and on water-gruel in an almshouse.... Was Thomas Paine here to-day his old remedies, religious and political *popular* free discussion and reasoning, would be thrown aside or only used to assist science and art to displace them in religious and state affairs." Truth will come to the surface! Here it is speaking for itself. The office of "art-liberty," the liberty for which infidels plead, is to destroy *popular free discussion* and *reasoning*, allowing them *only* in order to destroy themselves, that is, allowing the infidels to use them to displace them in RELIGIOUS and STATE *affairs*. This is called "art-liberty;" liberty in art and science, and despotism in religion and politics OR STATE. Such a society, plus the absence of conscience, virtue and vice, is the infidel's ideal of free government. All this means is simply "intolerance" by law; intolerance in "religious and state affairs."

When such a state of society is brought about in this country the infidels will have more *hell* than they will relish. Listen once more, "Man's right to be self-governed is, equally with his desire to be so, *self-evident*." How are these infidels going to have self-government and intolerance by law in matters of religion and state? This Godless infidel says, "But what is most insultingly *termed* 'elective franchise' is the farthest thing possible from self-government.... The *popular* free discussion of affairs of the last degree of complication, religious and state affairs, except during the *crisis* period of revolution, only renders that worst of despotisms, anarchy, chronic; it seats in the social organism that political gangrene, demagogism, which has always hitherto sooner or later required the cauterization of [104] military despotism in order to save even civilization. Despotism is the most inveterate of all the diseases of the social organism which ignorance has inflicted; nay, it is a complication of all its diseases. What, my fellow-man, would any of you think of the physician who should consult with an individual organism with a view to taking that organism's opinion as to what course he (the physician) had best pursue in order to cure him (the organism) of scrofula, complicated with every other bodily disease to which flesh is heir?... Evidently, church and state management require art and skill infinitely superior to what 'supernaturalism' and its legitimate child monarchism, or its bastard issue, caucus-and-ballot-boxism, are capable of. From the dissecting-room, the chemical laboratory, the astronomical observatory, the physician's and physiologist's study—in fine, from all the schools of science and arts should human law be *declared,* instead of being 'enacted' in legislative halls by those who in every respect besides political trickery, fraud and 'smartness,' are perfect ignoramuses." How is all this to be reconciled with the ideas of self-government set forth by this author and copied in this article? Who are to be the doctors, and who are to be the patients? When *popular* discussion is confined to art and science, only as it may be used in order to keep it out of religious and state affairs, who are to be the *popular* free disputants? When legislative halls are done away, along with their *progenitors,* elective franchise and representation, and law emanates from all the schools of science and art by "declaration," will men be more ready to obey?

Give the sore-headed, politically gangrened, conscienceless, virtueless, Godless applauders of Tom Paine what they ask, and it will simply amount to abandoning our posterity to the lowest, vilest sensualism known in Pagan geography along the line or borderland of a foul lust-gratifying, brutalizing *hell.* May all Christian people, and every lover of our humanity, wake up to the importance of giving these wide-mouthed, blatant infidels, who are traveling over our country howling about "liberty of man, woman and child," a wide berth. They would like to be the "doctors," and treat the "orthodox" people so as to purge "*popular* free discussion" out of them, and at the same time have their own stomachs crammed full of that grace, and so "steal heaven's livery to serve the devil." The above *infidelism* is copied *verbatim* from the "concluding application" of the life of Thomas Paine by Calvin Blanchard, published in 1879, and being now peddled over our country. What do our infidel friends mean by so much ado about liberty as opposed to the present state of society in our country? Free thought belongs to all. You can't chain the mind. What is it that they want? Will they be so kind as to inform us? Is Calvin Blanchard a representative of the liberty sought for? Then may we long live to keep our heels upon it.

Did The Race Ascend From A Low State Of Barbarism?

The fact that the human mind abhors a contradiction is an evidence of the Godlike nature of man, and an objection to the old tenet of total depravity; it is also the secret of the effort, upon the part of errorists, to systematize. One assumption creates a demand for another, and thus men who start wrong, in science or religion, labor under great disadvantages. When an idea is once consecrated to science or religion in the human heart it is hard to eradicate. When you find that you have made a wrong start remember that it is the part of true manhood to make a frank surrender, and start anew.

The assumption of the "evolution of species" lays all its advocates under the necessity of assuming that a low state of barbarism lies behind the civilization known in the history of the race as the primitive or first condition of intellect. Now, as this is a question of fact, an examination of the evidence pertaining to this second assumption is a matter of primary [106] importance. What are the facts bearing upon the question? With Darwinians the "primeval savage" is a stereotyped idea, finding expression in every-day language; and an idea that some scientists (rather sciolists) never get tired of promulgating. With them primitive man was little removed from the brute beasts, devoid of knowledge, art, and language—a creature in a small degree above; and in a great degree below, the anthropoid apes, from whom it is claimed he has descended by evolution. Is there any proof of this primitive inferiority, or savagery, as opposed to civilization? How does the voice of history speak? It doubtless shows many instances of improvement, of an advance from a low condition to a higher one; but what does the earliest history say as respects the *primitive condition of mankind*? Waiving an examination of the Bible history, we will at once proceed to other sources. In Egypt there are no indications of an early period of barbarism. All authorities agree that we find no rude or heathenish time in the far off history of Egypt out of which civilization was evolved. The first king known in Egyptian history, Menes, changes the channel of the river Nile, makes a great reservoir, and erects the Temple of Phthah at Memphis. His son Athothis is known as the builder of the Memphite Palace, and as a physician, who wrote books on anatomy. The pyramid times are early in Egyptian history; the portrayed scenes in the tombs of this early period reveal the same habits which existed in after times. That writing had been long in use is demonstrated by the hieroglyphics in the Great Pyramid. Go as far back as you may in Egyptian history, you will find no primitive barbarous mode of life. Sir Charles Lyell admitted, in "Antiquity of Man," p. 90, that "we have no distinct *geological evidence* that the appearance of what are called the inferior races of mankind has always preceded in chronological order that of the higher races."

[107]

George Rawlinson says Mr. Pengelly made a similar confession at the meeting of the British Association at Bristol, in August, 1875. So far as this question of evolution is concerned, it is just as easy to establish involution of civilization into barbarism as evolution of civilization out of barbarism. Herodotus gives an account of the Geloni, a Greek people, who were driven from the cities on the northern coast of the Euxine, and retiring into the interior, lived in wooden huts, and used a language half Scythian and half Greek. We follow this people down to the times of Mala and find them fully barbarous, using the skins of those slain in battle as coverings both for themselves and their horses. The Copts, of our times, are degraded descendants of the ancient Egyptians. In North and South America the descendants of the Spanish conquerers are poor representatives of those Castilians who, under Pizarro and Cortez mastered the Peruvian and Mexican kingdoms, and planted the civilization of the old world in the new. Civilization is liable to decay, to wane, to deteriorate, to sink so low that it may be a question whether it is any longer civilization. In the cases we have alluded to we have a low degradation retaining evidences of something higher. In comparative philology we have cases where it is presumed by the best of critics that a higher state of civilization sank to the lowest conceivable state of heathenism. The race existing in Ceylon, known as the "Weddas," is of this type. The language of the Weddas is regarded as a base descendant of the most complete and first known form of Aryan speech, the Sanskrit; and the Weddas are set down as descendants of the Sanskritic Aryans, who conquered India. There are no savages of a more debased type. They do not count beyond two or three; they have no idea of letters; of all the animals the dog alone is domesticated; their art consists in making bows and arrows and constructing rude huts; they are dwindling and threaten to become extinct. See "Report of the British Association for the advancement of science, for the Year 1875," part 3, p. 175.

Civilization and barbarism are states between which men oscillate, passing from one to the other with equal ease, according to the influences brought to bear upon them.

The mythical traditions of almost all peoples place at the [108] beginning of the history of the race, a "golden age," which is the opposite of savagery and barbarism. The Chinese speak of a "first heaven," an age of innocence and a state of happiness, when "all was beautiful and good, and all beings were perfect." Mexican tradition speaks of the golden age of Tezcuco; and Peruvian history commences with two "Children of the Sun," who established civilization on the borders of Lake Titicaca. The Greeks described their golden age as follows:

"The immortal gods, that tread the courts of heaven,

First made a golden race of mortal men.
Like gods they lived, with happy, careless souls,
From toil and pain exempt; nor on them crept
Wretched old age, but all their life was passed
In feasting, and their limbs no changes knew.
Nought evil came them nigh; and, when they died,
'Twas but as if they were o'ercome by sleep.
All good things were their portion; the fat soil
Bare them its fruit spontaneous, fruit ungrudged
And plentiful; they, at their own sweet will,
Pursued in peace the tasks that seemed them good,
Laden with blessings, rich in flocks, and dear
To the great gods."—*Hesiod.*

Such is the light that shines from the region where myth and history meet and wed. Can we go beyond this? There is no people, east or west, characterized by an uninterrupted *progress* from barbarism to civilization. So the theory of time based upon such an idea is altogether without foundation.

The Flood Viewed From A Scientific And Biblical Standpoint.

Unbelievers usually pass over the events of the flood with mockery. There is something about them that is only reconcilable with the mental condition of the man who says in his heart, "There is no God." The old methods of their interpretation of the Scriptures have been abandoned in many particulars.

This is the result of two things: first, progression in scientific knowledge; and, second, the Bible was always ahead of science in its scientific allusions. Now, it is known to scientists that there is, at the lowest calculation, forty-eight times more water in our seas and oceans than Keill was willing to allow when he made the objection that it would require the waters of twenty-eight oceans to give us Noah's flood. The objection was, "there is not water enough." Men seemed to think that the earth contained the water; that the water was standing in the earth. This was very natural, for people generally live upon the land. The Bible, however, presented a different idea, saying, the earth was "standing out of the water and in the water."

When the Scriptures speak upon this subject they refer to the waters just as a man would who never had any misgivings upon the subject of their sufficiency. Their teachings are in harmony with recent scientific discovery, and against old-fashioned unbelief.

Before Galileo's time men would have been regarded insane if they had asserted the gravity of the air, but the Bible contained the fact. It was laid away in Job 28: 25: "For he looketh to the ends of the earth and seeth under the whole heaven to make the weight for the winds; and he weigheth the waters by measure."

The force that is required annually in nature to give us the upper waters, to form the clouds, is estimated by Arago to be more than the labor of four hundred million of able bodied men, continued two hundred thousand years.—*Aunuaire du bur. des. longit.*, 1835, p. 196.

The Scriptures speak of floods and disorders that unbelievers of the bygone considered incredible, but in the present time geologists feel that the half was not told, for they are unable to account for all the destructions found in their investigations. The events known in the geological history are only in harmony with the fact that our planet has been subjected to immense submersions. They are scientifically described thus: An internal

[110]

fire which, raising the temperature of the seas and of the deep waters, caused on the one side an enormous evaporation and impetuous rains, as if the flood-gates of heaven were opened; and, on the other, an irresistible dilation, which not only raised the waters from their depths, broke up the fountains of the GREAT ABYSS, and raised its powerful waves to the level of the highest mountains, but which caused immense stratifications of calcareous carbonate, under the double pressure of a great heat and a pressure equal to eight thousand atmospheres.—*Gansen,* p. 195.

The same author gives us the following, which will be beneficial to the scholar: "Water is dilated 1-23 in passing from the temperature of ice melting to that of water boiling. An elevation of from sixteen to seventeen degrees Reaumer will then increase its volume 1-111. Now, we find by an easy calculation that the quantity of water necessary to submerge the earth to the height of 1-1000 of the radius of our globe is equal to 1-333 of its entire volume, or 1-111 of its third. If, then, we suppose that the one third of the terrestrial globe is metallic (at the mean specific gravity of 12-1/2), that the second third is solid (at the weight of 21), and that the remaining third is water; then, first, the specific gravity of the entire globe will be equal to 5-1/2 (according to the conclusions of Maskeline and of Cavendish); and, secondly, it will have been sufficient for the submersion of the earth to the height of 6,368 metres, or 1,546 metres above Mount Blanc; that the temperature of the mass of the water in the days of the deluge should have risen to sixteen degrees Reaumer is a reasonable conclusion." This calculation also has reference to the unnecessary idea that the flood was universal. But why is it that a few men recognize the existence of a God omnipotent and ridicule the flood?

The sufficiency of the ark is also called in question. Buffon says the various species of four-footed animals may be reduced to two hundred and fifty. And Dr. Hales shows conclusively that the ark had the capacity of bearing forty-two thousand four hundred and thirteen tons. He says: Can we doubt of it being sufficient to contain eight persons and about two hundred and [111] fifty pair of four-footed animals, together with all the subsistence necessary for twelve months, with the fowls of the air and such reptiles and insects as can not live in water? Besides places for the beasts and birds and their provisions, Noah might find room in the third story for thirty-six cabins occupied by household utensils, instruments of husbandry, books, grains and seeds, for a kitchen, a hall, and a space of about forty-eight cubits in length to walk in. In addition to all this, it is conceded, by the very best minds conversant with ship building, that Moses' description of the dimensions of the ark are the descriptions of one of the very best floating vessels that ever rested upon the waters. This fact has puzzled the minds of many unbelievers who seem to think there was but little scientific knowledge in that early period. They do not believe that God was with Noah. HE WAS.

The Mosaic Law In Greece, In Rome, And In The Common Law Of England.

There is no logical reason against the thought that God gave to man law in the gift of speech or language. Speech is not natural to man. He does not express his feelings and passions with sighs and groans systematically and invariably as do the lower animals. The speechless child has no order of this kind; the lower kingdom differs widely from man in this respect; the same animals have the same manner of expressing their feelings and passions throughout the world; but man has language to express *ideas*. Infants learn to speak by imitation; they do not speak naturally. Language is the result of education, of the imitative faculty of man. "It has been experimentally demonstrated that a man who has never heard the articulations of the human voice can never speak." So deafness always carries dumbness along with it when that deafness is from birth, or contracted in early childhood. I have in my mind at the present moment two bright-eyed girls in their "teens," who contracted deafness in infancy from the spotted fever; both are destitute of speech. If there ever was a language of nature it was abandoned when artificial language was taught. The greatest philosophers have failed to account for the origin of language or speech. The Pagans have declared that it was a gift from the gods. If all the inhabitants of the world could be congregated, and all would consent to the use of one and the same vocabulary, then we might, through universal training in that vocabulary, have an universal language. How could such a convention be assembled? The truth is, the origin of language or speech is neither natural or conventional, but imitative, and it is a fact, beyond the possibility of cavil, that the thing must have existed before it could have been imitated. With whom did it exist? "We think by words, and infants think by things." Words were from God.

[112]

Two lessons we must have as a capital to work with, and all else that we need will grow legitimately out of exercise in those two. "First, The elementary ideas. Second, The elementary words significant to them." Such was doubtless given man, as the Bible teaches, as a capital stock, and all languages are, directly or indirectly, from this original stock, and its results upon the human understanding; for who can set limits to possibilities of the human mind when once it is furnished with a capital stock and learned the art of its use? In Europe twenty-seven languages are known, which are kindred branches from three roots, and these three roots are scions of one stock; all languages are traceable to one stock. The Bible *alone* accounts for the origin of speech, which was, doubtless, the origin of law. Chaldea, Media, Persia, Phœnicia and Egypt, under the sovereignty of Chedorlaomer, had everything in legislative knowledge to learn from the Hebrews. This "Chedorlaomer was king of Elam, in Persia, in the times of Abraham. He made the cities in the region of the Dead Sea his tributaries; and on their rebelling he came with four allied kings and overran the whole country south and east of the Jordan. Lot was among his captives, but was rescued by Abraham." *See Zell's Encyclopedia.* Lycurgus, a celebrated legislator of Sparta, [113] who was born 926 years before Christ, gave an agrarian law that finds its prototype, without its defects, in the agrarian law of the Hebrews. Solon, one of the seven wise men of Greece, who died 558 years before Christ, transcribed, from the laws of Moses, the laws prohibiting certain degrees in marriage. The laws of descent, among the Grecians, are almost identical with the laws of descent among the Jews. The Grecians borrowed many laws from the Hebrews. They had their harvest vintage festival; the presentation of the best of their flocks; the offering of their first fruits, and the portion prescribed to their priests; the law against garments of divers colors; protection from violence to the man who fled to their altars; the law prohibiting all from the altar who had touched a dead body or any other impurity; the law prohibiting from the priesthood all those having blemishes upon their persons. All these laws, found in the Athenian code, had their origin with the laws of the Hebrews—were taken from Moses.

During the reign of Artaxerxes Longimanus, who was the brother of Darius, and who ascended the throne of the kingdom of Persia in the year 465 before Christ, the Jews were scattered all over the kingdom of Persia, and their laws were the subject of conversation and notoriety. Haman speaks of them to the king as differing from the laws of all other people.

The oldest and most noted legislators and wise men took their laws from the law of Moses. The Egyptians and the Phœnicians borrowed from the Jewish laws. Ancient and modern writers affirm that the individuals commissioned by the Senate and tribune under Justinian to form the "Twelve Tables" were directed to examine the laws of Athens and the Grecian cities. This took them at once to the consideration of many of the laws of Moses. Zell, in his Encyclopedia, says: The glory of Justinian's reign is the famous digest of the Roman law, known generally as the Justinian code, which was compiled out of the Gregorian, Theodorian and Hermogenian codes, by ten of the ablest lawyers of the empire, under the guiding genius of the Jurisconsult Tribonian. Their labors consisted, first, of the "Statute Law." Second, The "Pandects," a digest of the decisions and opinions of former magistrates and lawyers. These two compilations consisted of matter that lay scattered through more than two thousand volumes, now reduced to fifty. Third, The "Institutes," an abridgement in four books, containing the substance of all the laws in the elementary form. Fourth, The laws of *modern date*, including Justinian's own edicts, collected into one volume and called the "New Code."

The word "Pandects" is a term of great importance in the investigation of the origin of the Roman laws; it points directly and certainly to the fact that the Roman laws, known as the *Pandects*, were gathered from all laws, for such is the import of the term itself when it is associated with the term *laws*. Moreover, it is a Greek term, showing at once that the Grecian laws contributed largely to the *Pandects* of the Roman laws. The term is defined by Liddel and Scott in the words, *all-receiving, all-containing*, so the *Pandects* were gathered from *all laws*, consequently from the laws of Moses as well as from the Grecian laws, which were largely from the laws of Moses. This relationship, existing in the science of law, between the laws of the Bible and the Roman laws gotten up under Justinian, can be set aside by the infidels when stubborn facts, as well as similitude, are set aside.

Sir Matthew Hale says: Among the many preferences which the laws of England have above others, the two principal ones are, the hereditary transmission of property and the trial by jury, which originated with the Jews, for, by the law of Moses, the succession in the descending line was to the sons, the oldest having a double portion. If the son died in his father's lifetime, the grandson heired the portion of his father. Trial by jury was first suggested in the administration of penal justice among the Jews. Such trials came off publicly in the gates of the city, and their judges were elders and Levites, taken from the general mass of the citizens. "A part of the common law, as it now stands, was first collected by Alfred the Great, youngest son of Athelwolf, [115] or Ethelwolf, King of the West Saxons, who took the crown in 871. It is asserted by Sismondi, in his history of the fall of the Roman Empire, that when the above named prince caused a republication of the Saxon laws he inserted several laws taken from the Judaical ritual into his statutes to give new strength and cogency to the principles of morality. So it is a common thing in the early English reports to find frequent references to the Mosaic law. Sismondi also states that one of the first acts of the clergy under Pepin and Charlemagne, of France, was to introduce into the legislation of the Franks several of the Mosaic laws found in the books of Deuteronomy and Leviticus. It is truthfully said that the entire code of civil and judicial statutes throughout New England, and throughout the States first settled by the descendants of New England, were the judicial laws of God as they were delivered by Moses. From God himself one nation, and one only, received their laws, and they are worthy of being regarded as models for all succeeding ages. The learned Michaelis, who was professor of law in the University of Gottingen, says that a man who considers laws philosophically, who would survey them with the eye of a Montesquieu, would never overlook the laws of Moses."

Goguet, in his learned treatise upon the origin of laws, says: The more we meditate on the laws of Moses the more we shall perceive their wisdom and inspiration. They alone have undergone no changes, amendments or retrenchments for more than three thousand years, while all others have been receiving amendments and additions.

Milman, in his history of the Jews, says: The Hebrew law-giver exercised a more extensive and permanent influence over the destinies of mankind than any other individual in the annals of the world. The late Fisher Ames, a distinguished statesman and jurist, said, "No man can be a sound lawyer who is not well read in the laws of Moses." The seat of this law is the bosom of God, and her voice is the order, peace and happiness of the world.

[116]

Did Adam Fall Or Rise?

The old scholastic ideas of "total hereditary depravity, and miraculous conversion," with their correllates, have driven more minds into doubt and skepticism than most of men are apprised of. The reasons are evident. First. Common sense shrinks from them as ideas which are destructive of every principle of human responsibility. Second. They are opposed to the testimony of consciousness which asserts the soul's freedom. Third. They are opposed to correct ideas of justice as it is administered in all governments, both human and divine.

"And the Lord God said, Behold, the man is become as one of us to know good and evil." Our fathers, of Calvinistic type of faith, used to tell us that this language only asserted Adam's experience of conscious guilt; that he knew good before he transgressed, and had experimental knowledge of evil after he transgressed. This was the best they could do and save their Calvinism, and even this would not have saved it in the days of investigation like ours. The Lord did not say, "The man is become as one of us knowing good and evil," but "the man is become as one of us *to know* good and evil." The old view of the subject virtually says, The Lord had experimental knowledge of both good and evil, and that the way in which Adam became Godlike was the way of the transgressor. Then the greatest Godlikeness is the result of the greatest sinning. *What nonsense!* The Bible says: "And the eyes of them both were opened, and they knew they were naked; and they sewed fig leaves together and made themselves aprons." The account also asserts that the "tree of knowledge of good and evil" was "a tree to be desired to make one wise." Total depravity and its correllates could never have been found in this context. This history is not responsible for it, nor for the mischiefs it has produced.

The Heavenly Father knew, when he created man, that he would fail upon trial. To have prevented this would have been nothing short of an interference with man's freedom, and [117] consequently his responsibility, without which he could not have been man. The Lord saw man in his alien state and in his return to holiness. He "made of one blood all nations of men to dwell upon all the face of the earth, and determined the times before appointed, and the bounds of their habitation, that they *should seek the Lord.*"—See Acts 17: 26. It was necessary that man should become as God *to know good and evil* in order that he might be continued upon trial in a world of good and evil. To this end the Divine Ruler placed in the test fruit, the fruit of the tree that was forbidden, a mental lever to endow man with wisdom as God to know good and evil, without which the man's responsibility in relation to good and evil could never have been.

The fruit of the tree of life was for man's physical nature; was to control the law of organic being, regulating waste and supply so as to prevent the present effects of old age, and keep man in perpetual conditions of youth. After man had sinned, with the knowledge of good and evil, he was master of his position, and now, lest he "put forth his hand and take of the tree of life, and eat and live forever," subjected to shame, to torment, to anguish and tribulation, mental suffering, a lost being in the state of abandoned fallen angels, with a possibility of corrupting his conscience until it should be past feeling, seared as with a hot iron, and so glory in his shame; or, otherwise, be beyond the motive power of life and the restraining power of death, the Infinite One placed him beyond the reach of the tree of life. All of these ways or doings of the Heavenly Father were right, were merciful, were best for man. THE WAYS OF GOD ARE RIGHT. THE WAYS OF GOD ARE BEST. Farewell to "total hereditary depravity, and farewell to all its necessary correllations, such as miraculous conversion," etc.

Man is mentally endowed with wisdom by the tree of the knowledge of good and evil; is kept from ruining himself forever by being placed beyond the reach of the tree of life; is continued upon trial in a world of good and evil; is responsible through his knowledge of good and evil, and the motive power of life, and the restraining power of death is preserved to control him for his own eternal good; and, blessed be the name of our Heavenly Father, his eyes are open; so if man goes to perdition he must go *with his eyes open.* In all this we have perfect harmony with all Bible duty and truth, and also with science and universal consciousness of freedom and ability to choose and act. Not by a hair's breadth has God ever infringed upon the freedom of the

[118]

soul to shape and mould its own moral character, and shape its own moral destiny; but he has done many wonderful things to better the condition of the free soul—not forsaking it in the hour of greatest need.

The soul's free, voluntary service is that which constitutes the requirement of religion in all the ages.

Did They Dream It, Or Was It So?

That there was such a person as Jesus Christ living in the land of Judea at the time allowed by all Christians is no longer disputed by unbelievers. That he lived a life far superior to the lives of all other men is also conceded. If the powers of life and death were under his control he was more than human. If he rose from the dead he was the Son of God. Did he rise? This is a question upon which the whole Christian scheme hinges. What was the nature of the fact? Was it one about which men could be mistaken? Was it a fact which, occurring, addressed itself to the senses? If it was the witnesses could not be mistaken. There is not a court in the universe that would allow it.

There are things about which wise men may be mistaken, but they are not things which address themselves to the senses. Those are things in which fools may not, can not, be mistaken. It is impossible for my wife to be mistaken about my presence at this moment, but it is just as possible as it was for any of the first witnesses of Christ's resurrection to be mistaken. They were not, they could not be mistaken. Then what becomes of Strauss's mythical idea. What folly it is to allow that those witnesses were [119] perfectly honest, enthusiastically and proverbially honest in all they said, and yet mistaken.

This moral honesty and enthusiasm which Strauss and others allow to the credit of the witnesses is undoubtedly designed as a feeler—a mere catering to the views of Christians upon the character of the first Christians. Very good fellows (?) after all. How is that? If one of my neighbors would go into a court room to-morrow and testify under oath that he was with me yesterday, and the court was in possession of the fact that I was not with him, or near him at all, would it allow honesty to the witness? Would not every sensible man say, in his heart, he is a perjured witness? If he was with Walker he knew it; and if he was not with him he knew it.

Gentlemen, exercise all your shrewdness, adopt Strauss's idea of a mythical origin of the gospel of Christ, both as respects his miracles, which were either seen or not seen, and as respects his resurrection, then spread the blanket of honesty and warm-hearted enthusiasm over those men who sacrificed everything, life not excepted, for the testimony which they bore, and the next day any well-instructed judge of our courts would say, it is nonsense; they could not be mistaken about any fact which addressed itself to their eyes and ears. Christ rose from the dead if the witnesses told the truth; and the witnesses told the truth if they were honest men; and if they were not honest, labor, toil, suffering and martyrdom are no evidences of sincerity.

Can you believe in harmony without believing in a harmonist?

Can you believe that all things in nature adjusted themselves to each other?

Can you believe that life, and mind, and moral nature, each and all came from where neither existed?

[120]

Miscellaneous.

Voltaire built a church to God at Ferney.

Can you believe that your great ancestors were apes?

Do you oppose the Bible and prefer its legitimate effects?

Huxley wants the Bible introduced into boarding schools.

Can you believe in design without believing in a designer?

Tyndal says the theory of evolution of species is utterly uncredited.

Can you believe that the type which made these letters set themselves up?

The *Saturday Review* says Hume used to go to church sometimes in Scotland.

Can you believe that mind is the result of blind, unintelligent, mechanical forces?

Tyndal says spontaneous generation is the one essential pillar of evolution of species.

Tyndal says the failures to produce spontaneous life by experimenting are lamentable.

Collins insisted on his servants going to church "that they might not rob or murder him."

Can you believe that worlds hung themselves together and move themselves, as one grand whole, through space?

Can you believe that the correllation of things in nature was without design? that such adaptations as light to the eye was unintended?

Can you be honest in exerting your influence against the religion of Jesus Christ while it is your candid conviction that a country is better off with it than without it?

Do you sometimes say you prefer to live where there are churches and Sunday-schools, and all their appliances for the bettering of the condition of humanity, and at the same time constantly find fault with the Bible and religion which creates such things? If such is your course, are you strictly honest?